THE LAWS OF
SUCCESS &
HAPPINESS

DR. FREDERICK BAILES
Business Counsellor
Lecturer
Vocational Analyst

Martino Publishing
Mansfield Centre, CT
2013

Martino Publishing
P.O. Box 373,
Mansfield Centre, CT 06250 USA

ISBN   978-1-61427-550-3

Cover design by T. Matarazzo

Printed in the United States of America On 100% Acid-Free Paper

THE LAWS OF
SUCCESS &
HAPPINESS

DR. FREDERICK BAILES
Business Counsellor
Lecturer
Vocational Analyst

ANYONE CAN HAVE SUCCESS

Success is not the gift of Providence to a favored few. Any average man or woman can achieve it under skilled teaching. It is a common mistake to think that the winner has something mysterious in his make-up, and that unless one has this indefinable "something" he can never get to the top. The world is full of ordinary men and women who have cashed in on their ordinary talents and made extraordinary success. But they never would have done this if they had sat with folded arms and said, "Well, if success were intended for me it would have come to me easily; as it is, I find it easier to fail than to succeed."

There is no essential difference between the man who succeeds and the one who fails. The difference lies in the methods they pursue. The winner uses winning methods. The loser uses losing methods. And it is just as hopeless for a person to try and succeed while using losing methods as it would be to try and swim while using walking methods.

Success is not an accident. It comes from following clearly defined laws that are as old as the universe. A few instinctively follow these laws, and make rapid and spectacular success. But whether consciously or not they are following the laws. John D. Rockefeller and Henry Ford are outstanding examples of this group. But the majority of men are not Rockefellers or Fords. They must learn, lesson by lesson, the steps which these famous men took in their march upward to the heights.

If the reader could interview thousands of successful men, and ask them for their formula of success, he could in time work out a series of principles by which these men have worked, and by following it could make a success of his own affairs. But the average man or woman has neither time nor the opportunity for doing this. The writer has interviewed successful men in every walk of life, and brings to you in this book their experiences boiled down to the practical point. By following the methods and principles, and by developing the very same attitude of mind which characterizes these men, any person of average intelligence can get away from the lower levels into the place in life for which he feels himself fitted.

THE MIND OF THE WINNER

One thing that distinguishes the winner from the loser is an attitude of mind. It is the purpose of this book to develop that mental attitude in the reader and student.

Mind is the most important thing in the universe. It was also the first thing that existed. Before any tangible thing existed — away back before our material world had its beginning — it was the Divine Mind. Gradually the outworking of that creative mind showed itself in the various forms of matter. A universe took shape and substance at the call of Mind. Everything we have today is an orderly unfolding of a plan conceived ages ago.

Our bodies show a similar plan. A male and a female cell came together and became one. It was so tiny that it could not be seen with the naked eye. Yet in that tiny cell, smaller than the smallest grain of dust, was wrapped up the man that was to be. The shape of the head, the color of the eyes and hair, the tilt of the nose, the line of the mouth, the quality of the voice, the kind of walk, the mental and emotional traits inherited from both parents, the sex of the child to be were all there. These gradually developed and unfolded under that universal plan for nine months in the mother's body, until a child was born who showed the outworking of those traits that were hidden away, wrapped up and sealed in that infinitesimal life cell. And throughout the life of that human being he will continue to unroll

9

various qualities which were present in that first life cell.

Mind lifted man above the remainder of creation. It distinguishes him from the brute. And every advance that has ever been made is a triumph of mind. Those who have stood a little higher than their fellows, from the first glimmering thinker of prehistoric days to the leader of the twentieth century, have stepped ahead because they learned to do something that the crowd had not yet learned to do. Hence the importance of understanding our own minds and letting them work for us.

THE TWO MINDS

Until recent times men studied the mind as a single unit. To them any mental state was a product of "mind." But keen students have come to see that mind is a complex thing, and that it sets certain parts to do entirely different kinds of work. This discovery has opened the way into an entirely new world; has given us access to hitherto undreamed of stores of mental power. It has done so much to give men success that William James of Harvard, the father of modern psychology, has said that the dis-

10

covery of the subconscious mind was the greatest discovery of the nineteenth century.

Scientists divide the mind into two parts, the conscious mind and the subconscious mind. The conscious mind is that part of the mind that prompts us to carry on activities of which we are conscious. When we decide to speak, sing, throw a ball, jump across a brook we do it in response to a prompting of the conscious mind. This is the division of the mind that is particularly active while we are awake. When we go to sleep it goes off the job. We are not conscious of the furnishings of the room, the pictures on the wall, the bed upon which we sleep. Yet our minds still work. The subconscious mind is building pictures which we call dreams. Mind is never totally inactive. People often insist that they never dream. Everybody dreams. Yet we remember only the dream which is with us shortly before we awake. Our subconscious is carrying us out into the dream-world every moment while we sleep. There is no person who never dreams, but there are people who never recall their dreams. And they are usually greatly offended when the scientist insists that they dream whether they recall it or not. Dreams are the working of the subconscious mind, that part of the mind which is below the level of consciousness. The sub-

11

conscious works while we are awake as well as asleep, as we shall see later. In fact these two divisions of the mind overlap; it is not always easy to see which work is being done consciously and which subconsciously.

THE GIANT WITHIN US

The subconscious is by far the more important side of our minds, the more powerful and extensive. Only five per cent of our mental work is done by the conscious mind, ninety-five per cent being done subconsciously. Like an iceberg, which has nine-tenths of its bulk beneath the surface of the ocean, the subconscious buried powers are the forces that bring success. The strength of the winner lies in the development of his buried powers. Herein lies the secret of success and health.

YOUR SECRET FORCES

The subconscious is the engineer of the body. Nothing goes on anywhere in the universe without mind. Our bodies do not build themselves. They are run by the subconscious mind, buried below the surface, like the engineer in a good hotel. We push

12

a button and get lights, turn a faucet and get hot water, and are so accustomed to getting these results that we are likely to assume that they just happen. Yet they depend upon the work of the engineer in the basement. If he should go off the job we would get no results from our button pushing and faucet turning. Similarly, our bodies do not run themselves. They are run by the subconscious mind. We breathe, our glands, kidneys and liver operate, the heart keeps the blood circulating normally, and we are so accustomed to these activities that we come to think they just happen. In reality they are carried on by the subconscious mind, the engineer of the body. Every cell of our bodies is taught by this mind just which particles of nourishment to select as it is carried by on the blood stream, different cells requiring different elements for growth and life. As soon as enough food is taken in to satisfy the needs of the body the subconscious shuts off desire for more. Its marvelous intelligence keeps the heart beating seventy-two times a minute, the lungs bringing in air eighteen times every minute whether we consciously think of it or not. If these activities had to be carried on by the conscious mind it would go hard with us when we became absorbed in a movie thriller. We would forget to breathe. We would die in our seats. Yet the subconscious carries on every activity of the body with marvelous smoothness and efficiency. The conscious mind would be driven crazy if it had to carry on for five minutes the diversified functions which the subconscious mind does with ease.

THE SECRET OF MEMORY

The subconscious is the seat of memory. It is the vast store house of knowledge. Every experience we have ever had from childhood until the present moment, is stored up and kept by the subconscious mind. We never forget a thing we have experienced. We look in a store window and move, remembering a particular gown or gun because it made a striking appeal to our conscious mind. Yet in reality the subconscious stored away the memory of every other gown or article we saw in that window. People are mistaken when they say they have poor memories. There are no poor memories. They may have difficulty in recalling, but not in storing away knowledge, because the subconscious does the latter with perfect ease. All memory systems are built upon this fact.

The secret of good memory lies in knowing how to command the subconscious to yield up stored knowledge. A drowning person sees his whole life sweep instantly in a panorama before him. Incidents from childhood which you could not have forced him to recall were handed up to him in that last moment. Where were those thoughts for years during his lifetime? Stored away safely in the subconscious.

The first experience I ever had with this remarkable ability of the subconscious was while getting surgical practice in London, England. Dr. Robert Burnett was a psychologist as well as a surgeon. We had operated upon a man; a few days later Dr. Burnett invited me to accompany him to the man's bedside in London Homeopathic Hospital. He placed the patient in a hypnotic state, and had him tell all the details of the operation. The man had been completely under the influence of the anaesthetic during the operation yet his subconscious had stored away that experience, and he repeated not only our actions but even long technical names of instruments called for during the operation. I have since done similar things many times in probing the subconscious.

RULES FOR MEMORY TRAINING

1. Let it make a definite impression. The more clearly you impress a thing upon the memory the easier to recall. Some people find that they can remember a thing better if they write it down. But the chief thing in making a definite impression is in-

terest. We recall the things we are interested in. Someone points out John Jones on the street. He is only a name to us and we forget him right away. But we meet Lindbergh and can recall every feature because we are intensely interested in him. The school-boy forgets his history dates, but can recall the football scores of twenty college teams because he is interested in football. Develop a genuine interest in the thing you want to remember, as a first step.

Attention enters into that first definite impression.

Attention means sidetracking everything else for the main thing. Shut everything else out of the mind while you concentrate on the thing to be remembered. The schoolgirl sitting on the beach trying to memorize Latin conjugations is whipped at the start. There is too much to distract the attention. Lock yourself in where you can bear down upon the thing to be remembered, until it makes a definite impression.

2. Associate it with something you know. Association makes memorizing easy. For example, in memorizing the names of the first seven Presidents, Washington, Adams, Jefferson, Madison, Monroe, Adams, Jackson, a good association system would be to make a sentence starting with the initial of the president. W.A.J.M.M.A.J. would fit "Wednesday

16

afternoon John met many American Jews." This sentence is more easily remembered than a lot of unconnected names.

3. Recall it several times. If it is the name of a person you have met it is good to call him by name two or three times during your conversation. Then at intervals during the days that follow recall his face and speak the name with it. Thus the face and name become associated together in the subconscious, and when one comes before you the other will come with it.

If you are trying to remember facts recall them at intervals. Practice reviewing every few hours for the first few days, and daily thereafter.

4. Don't worry. Trust your subconscious. When you worry you will not be able to remember a thing you are blaming the subconscious. You show that you do not trust it. The subconscious always works better when you praise it. Don't say "I have such a poor memory." Say "My memory is improving right along."

The subconscious is commanded through strong suggestions. Don't try to force it. Suggest to it. When we become tense and strained trying to recall a thing we are suggesting to the subconscious that it cannot recall for us. When we quietly trust it we

17

are giving it suggestions of confidence and it responds. How often have you struggled unsuccessfully with a name or a fact, but as soon as you gave up and said, "Oh, well, I'll leave off trying. It'll come back to me," the subconscious, realizing that the strain was off brought it up and said, "Here it is."

HARNESSING THE GIANT WITHIN

The subconscious is a giant compared to which the conscious is a pigmy. Yet the subconscious is the servant of the conscious. It can be controlled and made to use its tremendous powers to solve our life problems. Its powers are vast. No one has ever yet released the full force of his subconscious power. Thomas Edison says that the average man DOES NOT use ten per cent of his real ability. Vast stores of strength and tremendous possibilities lies buried beneath the surface of every one of us waiting to be released. We get hints of it now and then in our longings for bigger and better things; in the feeling that if we only had a chance we could make big success. Every wish and aspiration is proof of buried powers waiting to be released. The only person who can never achieve success is the man who has never felt the urge to do something big. The desire for success is the guarantee of success. All this subconscious power lies waiting for the word of the master. Self-mastery is simply training our conscious mind to control the servant through positive thinking. The trouble with many people is that they have allowed the subconscious to become the master. It is a poor master because it never reasons. Conscious mind is reasoning mind. It has the power of choice. It can choose to drop out of the mind all attitudes of discouragement, gloom, sickness, failure and practice the positive attitude of confidence, optimism, courage, aggressiveness, health.

The subconscious cannot choose, cannot reason. It looks to the conscious to protect it from error. Its function is to accept what the conscious gives it, then to carry out that thought like a blind servant in the body and mind. When it is allowed to assume the mastery in affairs of judgment it is lost, and life becomes a failure. The successful man uses its tremendous force, but keeps it in its place, by using the method outlined later in this book.

BUILDING HEALTH

The subconscious is the builder of the body, its health, character, courage, achievement or the opposite. It builds for good or evil, never reasoning out

19

the results, simply following the suggestions that are sent to it by the conscious.

Our bodies are made up of trillions of tiny cells. Some of these cells are dying every minute and new cells are being rebuilt to take their place, so that our whole body is completely rebuilt once a year. Every new cell is built by the subconscious mind. And the kind of cell it becomes is determined by the kind of thinking we do.

If we think morbid, unhealthy, sick thoughts the subconscious will reproduce these thoughts in our bodily tissues. If we think gloomy, depressing, fearful, cowardly thoughts the subconscious builder will build that kind of mental attitude, and failure will be the inevitable result.

A woman reproduces a fanciwork design by embroidering one little stitch at a time, while watching the pattern from which she is working. When sufficient stitches have been made she has worked an exact reproduction of that pattern. Each stitch may seem to be a small, unimportant thing, yet their total is a definite thing. In the same way the thoughts that we think are the pattern upon which the subconscious builds for failure or success. As long as we allow our conscious minds to dwell upon failure, or to entertain defeated thoughts, it is impossible for the subconscious to build that deep undercurrent of faith in ourselves which every successful man has. Each little thought, seemingly unimportant in itself, becomes a stitch in the pattern of life, and is reproduced with remarkable faithfulness by the subconscious mind. And gradually we lose the sense of mastery, our confidence wanes, and we build for ourselves a weak, negative character from the pattern placed daily before the subconscious through our conscious thinking.

THE LAW OF ATTRACTION

It is a law of the mind that we attract that which we fear, love or steadily expect. The reason for this is that we make clearer mental pictures of these things. The person who lives in fear of a certain happening finds that thing intruding itself upon his thoughts in a clear, distinct picture at frequent intervals. The man who is looking forward with fondness to his annual vacation finds himself making mental pictures of its various details even when he should be applying himself to his work. And all of us who hold steady expectations of some particular thing find that it comes to us unbidden, and always in a clear mental image.

Our mental world is as real as our material world. Everything we have was first formed within our mind. Our outer circumstances are but a reflection of our steady thinking.

There is a constant stream of thought flowing through our consciousness. A succession of thought pictures, with constantly changing forms. This is marked in what we usually call day-dreaming. That is, our minds lazily form one picture after another, and drift on from one to another, without any actual noticeable effort.

These constantly changing thought images produce no steady result because they are always on the move. They are not sharply defined — have no clearness. And the hazy, ever changing thought forms produce no permanent result because they are the result of scattered consciousness.

This scattered consciousness is a pitiable thing. Insanity is just an extreme case of this kind. The insane person babbles on about one thing after another, without coherence or logic. He cannot keep his attention in any one place. It is caught by every passing fancy, like a child's. On the other hand, every person who has made his mark has developed the power of concentration, the very opposite of scatterisation. Steady thinking produces steady action. Muddy thinking brings muddy action.

ATTRACTING SICKNESS

During one of my classes on Health and Self-Mastery given in the Chamber of Commerce, Seattle, Washington, early this year a lady came to me with what her doctor had diagnosed as cancer of the breast. She had a hard, painful lump that had been developing visibly for over a year. I discovered that her mother and grandmother had died of cancer. That all her life she had lived in a horror of cancer. That every ache and pain, every bump she received had suggested cancer to her. That fear picture of cancer held steadily before the subconscious mind had been a cancer pattern. The subconscious had actually built diseased cells one by one. There is not one disease that cannot be reproduced in this way. I gave her a course of mental training, and in five weeks that lump had disappeared.

While I was lecturing in Kansas City a banker was committed to prison for misappropriation of funds. The shame was so great that he said, "I never want to come out alive." He was a healthy man, with no trace of organic weakness when he entered the prison, but in three months of that destructive kind of thinking he broke down and died from nothing but worry and the desire to die.

There is a very splendid group of Roman Catholics

who have a devotional exercise called "Contemplating the Wounds of Jesus." They spend long periods gazing upon the picture of the crucified Christ. And this loving contemplation, steadily pursued, brings out the finest feelings of gratitude and devotion. But in over one hundred fully authenticated instances the thinking of these devout men and women has actually produced scars on face or hands similar to those made by the nails or the thorns. And in one notable instance — that of St. Francis of Assisi — the scar tissue in the hands was so lifelike that the undertaker tried to pull them out after death, thinking it was actual nail-heads.

THINKING FOR HEALTH

If steady, concentrated thinking can produce unnatural effects like these mentioned in the three cases above, how much encouragement sick people can take. These results were effected through a natural law of the mind. That same law will operate much more quickly and surely in the direction of health, because health is natural while sickness is unnatural. Sickness was never intended for any of us. We become sick when we violate laws of the body through incorrect diet or bodily hygiene. We build diseased areas when we violate the laws of right thinking.

Let the sick person get a good clear picture of the organ or part that is faulty. Constantly picture that part as clean, healthy and well, entirely free from ache or pain. Hold steadily to that picture regardless of the way he feels. And by a natural law of the mind he can rebuild his body. No one can ever say his disease is incurable. It may be from the standpoint of medicine. Because medicine has its limitations. But after physical means have failed, and the patient given up to die, he can be cured, in a great many cases. The writer was given up to die of diabetes and is well and vigorous today, by correct eating and correct thinking. That is the reason he is on the lecture platform today instead of sitting in an office prescribing medicine. He has lectured to over three million people in the past ten years, on health and success.

THINKING FOR SUCCESS

Suppose one wants a winning disposition, free from "the blues." He should, in addition to following the practical rules laid down in later chapters, constantly hold the picture of himself as happy and free from worry.

If one wants more money, a better job, a happy marriage, more courage and determination, he should hold that picture steadily. Because we attract what we love and steadily expect. Most people can imagine anyone else but themselves succeeding in money, love or happiness. They think it too good to be true that they themselves should get these things, because they have been so long without them. They imagine that those achievements are for some lucky person — but not for them. According to your faith be it unto you. Heaven plays no favorites. We get what we go after. Each of us can be the lucky one.

This is not the whole program. But it is a beginning. And the person who starts now to apply this principle will begin to get results very soon. To think you can is to create the force that can.

HOW TO PRACTICE CONCENTRATION

A sun glass held steadily over a paper will burn a hole. But moved here and there constantly over the paper will get no results. Our minds are a sun glass. The stream of thought pouring through them are the rays that produce results.

Practice holding the mind steady by fixing the attention upon the small second hand of a watch. Bring it back every time it wanders. If you can hold the attention steadily for fifteen seconds you are not hopeless. If you can do it for thirty seconds you are fairly good. When you can do it for one minute you are getting self mastery. And two minutes is very good. Two minutes morning and evening steadily fixed upon your biggest desire in life will be a tremendous help in bringing it to pass.

Choose the same time, if possible, every day. Don't let ANY outside thought come in no matter how seemingly important. Every time the attention wanders force it back to the second hand. Soon you will find a new strength of will in focussing and bearing down upon any problem.

As a preparation it might be good to think over all the things which are likely to intrude themselves while you are concentrating. Thoughts of business, home, finance, duties, worries, joys, etc. Let them all pass quietly in review. Then say to yourself, "What am I going to do?" "I am going to practice concentration." "Then I will CONCENTRATE. So, good morning, every one of you outside thoughts. I will attend thoroughly and carefully to you when I get through. But for the next few minutes outside you go." This helps clear the mind.

SUGGESTION AND AUTO-SUGGESTION

Suggestion is the interflow between the conscious and the subconscious mind. It is any influence that changes the mind from one state to another.

There is nothing mysterious or uncanny about suggestion. It is merely the working of one of the laws of the mind. A boy has a toothache, but a circus parade goes by and his toothache has gone. That is suggestion. The baby falls and bumps its head. The parent kisses the sore spot and baby stops crying right away — that is suggestion. A neighbor comes in and tells you all about her troubles, pouring them into you for an hour. After she has gone you are blue and depressed — that is suggestion. A smiling, happy-faced friend stops to chat for a few minutes. After he has gone you feel that the world is a good place to live in — that is suggestion. Mix with lazy, un-ambitious, discouraged people and you find it easy to be the same — that is suggestion. Associate with refined, clean-minded, ambitious people and you find your own ideals soaring — that is suggestion.

Suggestions may come from others, or from within ourselves. When they come from within it is called auto-suggestion. When Emil Coue instructed sick people to say, "Day by day in every way I am growing better and better," he was teaching them one method of auto-suggestion.

The law of suggestion is the law of repetition. The thought suggested may be true or false, but if it is repeated often enough the subconscious mind will reproduce it in the life. People sometimes tell a lie often enough until they come to believe it themselves. Remember, the subconscious does not reason. It is merely the servant, blindly carrying out the orders of the conscious mind. All it needs is to receive the suggestion; then it proceeds to carry out that idea in the life, never reasoning whether it is a good or a bad suggestion. Every thought we accept passes down into the subconscious factory and is made over into bodily fiber or mental attitude.

HOW TO RESIST NEGATIVE THOUGHTS

Any thought that is allowed to pass unchallenged in the mind becomes part of the pattern of life. This is worked into the character, and nothing can stop it. If we allow negative or destructive ideas to lodge in the mind we will become that kind of a person. The average individual has spent the biggest part of his life telling himself he is no good, that he cannot do this or accomplish that. The fact is that he may be perfectly competent to do these things, but as long as he keeps thinking that he cannot he will be unable to do them. Never say a thing about yourself that you would not want to see come true.

Don't allow others to say things to you that suggest any inferiority. For example, don't allow others to call you a fool, even in fun. By the time you have accepted that suggestion a few times the subconscious is making it a part of the pattern of life. Our friends often say destructive things in fun. But the subconscious doesn't know it is in fun. It accepts the idea, with destructive results in our minds. We don't have to make a fuss with friends who have said such things in a spirit of banter. But we can throw off their bad effects by the use of a formula of four magic words. The moment they have given us any negative suggestion we can smile at them, and say under our breath the formula, which is "I RESIST THAT SUGGESTION." By so doing we have exercised the power of choice that lies in the conscious mind. No thought becomes a part of us until we have accepted it, and this deliberate rejection of negative ideas proves that we are making a definite choice of positive ideas.

HOW TO OVERCOME SENSITIVENESS

Some people are very sensitive. They are easily hurt by thoughtless things their friends or loved ones say. And sometimes people say things to us with the deliberate intention of hurting us. You can take the sting out of these things by instantly thinking, "I resist that suggestion." Don't stop to turn the destructive thought over in your mind. It gets a lodgment very quickly. Instantly resist it and throw it off.

Nobody can ever rob you of happiness without your consent. It does not matter how mean people are, nor what things they say to us or about us, we carry with us our own fire extinguisher that can instantly put out the fire. Many sensitive people play with the hurtful suggestions given them by others, brooding over the injustice of them until they are made miserable. The successful man has no time to accept these suggestions. People used to marvel at the way Theodore Roosevelt could smile into the face of his worst enemy, and be unaffected by the harsh things his opponent was saying to him. Roosevelt had mastered this secret of resisting negative suggestions. There is no copyright on it. Anyone can use it. It does not take will power. Merely a quick turn of the mind, and any undesirable thing is thrown off like water off a duck's back.

31

STEPPING ALONG WITH THE WINNERS

Students whom I have had for private instruction have often said, "Yes, I know that I should think the positive things. But I have thought negatively for so long that these thoughts just naturally rush in and overwhelm me, in spite of my desire to be positive. This discourages me and I feel like quitting."

The secret of positive thinking lies in the power of choice possessed by the conscious, reasoning mind. We can't help negative, discouraged thoughts coming to us even though we don't want them. They will come to us for a time. But gradually we will get our mind turned around, so that it automatically closes itself against the negative and opens to the positive suggestion as a habit. This is not done in a day. But there will be a change within a few days, and then it is only a matter of watching for positive ideas to select, until we wake up some morning to the realization that we have formed the positive habit. And that it is now much easier to stay on a happy level, instead of being up on the mountain top one day and down in the dark valley the next.

OVERCOMING THE BLUES

We cannot help the crows from flying over our houses, but we can chase them off before they build their nests in the eaves. So with negative suggestions. We can always choose to place a positive thought in front when the negative is knocking at the door. Thoughts always come in pairs. A negative thought can never come without a positive being alongside it. Suppose you wake up in the morning feeling unaccountably blue. Drive out that negative thought by choosing its positive opposite. Repeat to yourself, "I resist that suggestion." "I CHOOSE to feel happy today." It is not a questiton of FEELINGS. It is a matter of CHOICE. Your feelings have nothing to do with it. Babies live according to their feelings. So do ignorant savages and lunatics. But intelligent, purposeful men and women make their advances in life by a series of definite choices. In other words, let your will master your feelings. Never let your feelings master your will.

It has been said that every great poem, work of art, or business achievement has been accomplished by a man with a headache. Meaning, of course, that if we consider our feelings all the time we will never make a success of anything. Those who have succeeded have had just as many temptations to give in

33

to their disability, their weakness, their cowardice, or their laziness. But they have gone on, in spite of a thousand physical and mental handicaps. Their conscious deliberate choice was the guide, — never their feelings. After all, success starts and finishes with self mastery. Plain, ordinary hard work will conquer any outward circumstance once we have overcome our own inertia.

GETTING THE SUCCESS HABIT

By a series of conscious, deliberate choices the subconscious is shown that it must follow orders and work out the thought that you choose. By and by it becomes a well trained servant that anticipates your desires. You find that you have developed the habit of positive thinking, and it becomes easier to think success than failure. Success is a habit, just as failure is.

THE SECRET OF SELF-CONFIDENCE

Let us suppose you want to tackle some bigger job than you have ever attempted. The suggestion comes, "I can't do it." Let me say that most big men feel a certain amount of hesitancy in tackling a hard thing. You are not alone, therefore, in your feeling.

The thing to do is disregard your feelings and say, "Yes, I can do that." Even though your timidity shrieks out that you cannot do it, and that you lie when we say you can do it, hold steadily to the thought that of course you can do it. Remember that courage is not the absence of fear, but the conquest of fear. Everyone experiences fear at times, but the successful man goes on in spite of that fear.

It is far better to tackle a hard thing and fail to accomplish it than never to tackle it through fear. The worst that can happen is that we may not bring the thing to pass. But that is not failure. Failure is sitting down afraid to start. Every moment we sit shivering and unwilling to start we are failures. The moment we have started the thing we are successes, regardless of the outcome of the venture. Success is an attitude, rather than an accomplishment. Of course, the man who is forever starting and never finishing is not a success. But as you develop the courage to tackle things you will find that you are able successfully to accomplish what you start out to do.

Get this thought firmly fixed in your mind, and things will begin to happen which once you would have thought impossible. Your life will begin to show results. One of the outstanding qualities of the go-getter is his tackling of things that the other fellow is afraid to try. Yet the other fellow has every bit as much latent ability, and could do the same things if he would launch himself with a confident determination. The go-getter is not a marvel. He is willing to try.

THOUGHTS ARE THINGS

One of the marvels of modern science is the demonstrated fact that all matter is constantly in motion. Science first proved that light, heat, sound, color were merely a series of waves or vibrations travelling at a terrific rate of speed. Then it went further to show that even the so-called solid things like rocks were composed of millions of tiny atoms. These were further subdivided into electrons, and now they have divided the electrons into ions, the tiniest particle of matter known. These ions are always in motion, travelling at inconceivable rates of speed, and having millions of collisions with each other every second within that rock. And the difference in the various rates of vibration determines what kind of matter they become.

This has paved the way for us to understand the nature of thought. Thoughts are very minute waves or vibrations travelling at a very high rate of speed. They do not remain in the brain, but travel out throughout the universe. In 1928 the psychological department of the University of Nebraska perfected a machine which registers the thought vibrations of people. The delicate thought waves striking a highly sensitized surface register a sound like the gentle pattering of rain upon a roof. Our thoughts bombard each other, and we absorb the thoughts of others with whom we are in contact.

GETTING IN TOUCH WITH OTHER MINDS

Our minds are like radio stations. We can send out thoughts to others, or can receive thoughts from others. Every thought that we think is received some time by someone else. Some people who are extremely sensitive to thought, like the Nebraska machine, have developed that power to catch these thoughts consciously. This is called mind reading. While some are especially gifted in the ability to catch the thoughts of others, everyone has at some time or other found himself doing it. For example, two people are sitting quietly in a room or driving along in an automobile. Neither is talking. Suddenly one says, "I wonder if Joe will bring the lawn mower back to us today." And the other exclaims,

"I was just thinking of that very thing." This is not a coincidence. It is an actual case of thought transfer. The thought has travelled from one to the other.

But most people catch the thoughts of others subconsciously. That is, they do not recognize the thoughts as they come in, yet they receive them all the same. As in the radio field, we are in tune with certain wave lengths of thought, and we catch either negative or positive thoughts. Negative thoughts have a low rate of vibration. Positive thoughts are rapid vibrations. The radio catches radio waves of the wave length it is tuned to. So does the human mind. Therefore we catch either helpful or hindering thoughts from others according to our own mental condition.

WHY WE "FEEL" HAPPY OR UNHAPPY

If we think such negative things as sickness, poverty, gloom, discouragement, failure, those thoughts go out and register in the minds of the same class of people. Thus we tune in with their minds and push them lower. At the same time we receive their program of thought, which helps to hold us down on that negative level. Like two drowning men we interlock our minds and go down together. On the other hand, when we think happy, courageous, healthy, optimistic success thoughts these go out in very rapid vibrations and help the strong person to be stronger. In turn we draw strength from their thought. In other words, we draw to ourselves the kind of things we think.

FEELING FOLLOWS ACTION

The room or the open air in which you are reading this book is flooded with unseen radio waves from stations all over the world. You cannot feel them because your body and brain are not planned to take them in. But you can easily prove their existence by getting a radio and tuning it to a certain wave length. Immediately the room will be flooded with these waves in the form of music.

In the same way we live amid innumerable thought waves. We are absorbing them every moment we live. Roger Babson says that only five per cent of the people in the United States are interested enough in success to make the necessary effort to get it. That means that ninety-five per cent of the thoughts with which we are surrounded are negative. This is one reason why most people settle down and accept failure. They don't know how to tune out the failure vibrations and tune in with the winners.

39

We want to be tuned in with the doers of the world, and to draw new power from them. How shall we do it? By deliberately CHOOSING to think the positive thought. Never mind how we feel. We may feel all out of sorts. In spite of our feelings we can say, "I choose to think positively. I choose high rate thoughts." Never forget that word choose. It is the key to power. Our feelings have nothing to do with our choice. We can choose the kind of feelings we want. It is a fundamental law of the mind, brought out clearly by James and the later psychologists, that "FEELING FOLLOWS ACTION." In other words, act in the way that you *want* to feel. The man who waits until he *feels* better or stronger before he acts better or stronger will never get results because it is opposed to this law of his mind. We cannot violate the laws of our minds and then expect them to bring us good results. The man who wants success must follow the methods of success. Act out the part of the man you want to be, and soon your feelings will follow suit. Then, and then only, will you feel inside as you want to feel.

IN TUNE WITH THE WINNER

By deliberately choosing to think positively we automatically raise our wave length, and tune in with successful people. We were on the wrong level to

40

catch their thoughts before. Now the situation has changed.

Perhaps in Los Angeles or New York a keen, successful man is fighting hard to put through a business deal, or to close a sale. He has stores of courage or he would not be successful. He is now calling up all his courage, his positiveness, his optimism and his ingenuity in this battle of brains. Every thought he thinks is sent out over his mental wireless. We who are tuned in to catch positive thoughts get strength from his successful fight. Indeed, we win with every great winner everywhere in the world.

You go to bed at night tired out with a problem upon which you have been racking your brains all day. Still it seems no nearer a solution. But dropping off to sleep in that positive frame of mind you remain in touch with the best minds of the universe. You are surprised when you "dream" the solution to your problem, or that you wake up with the correct answer to it. There need be no surprise, now that you know this law of the mind. For the keenest minds of the universe have been helping you as you slept. The grumbler and the failure get none of this assistance. Those thought waves are for everyone, but only they get them who are tuned to catch them.

This is the secret of mental help. I have often been asked to help my students and clients in working out their problems, because two minds working consciously on the same level together can get double results. It would take a book as large as an encyclopedia to relate particular instances along this line.

GETTING A BETTER JOB

The man who wants a better job, or a bigger salary, must first think that thing. He must learn to put away those petty little appraisals of himself that have kept him on the fringe of poverty. He must learn to think highly of himself. If he thinks of his abilities as not worth much he will be on the same mental level with employers who think in the same way. And he simply will not register with the man who wants someone to whom he can pay a large salary.

If he dares to think highly of himself, and to value his services at a proper price, he will register on men tuned to think on the same price level. When he applies for a position with that kind of employer he will sense the mental union. Employers go on facts when hiring employees. But they go largely upon their own mental reaction to the various applicants for a position.

A young lady of ability took private work with me during a series of lectures in Denver. I drilled her in the idea that she had not been asking enough for her services. She had never earned above $18 a week. I schooled her in the idea that she was worth at least $40 a week. At first she said that was too much, because friends with more education were getting less than that. I pointed out that others with less education were getting more than that. In a week she got an offer of $27.50 a week and was delighted. I said, "Turn it down" and she was almost in tears. Reluctantly she refused this offer, but in less than two weeks afterwards she secured a position at $45 a week, which has been greatly increased since that time. Her employer later told me that he didn't know exactly why he selected her from among the other applicants, but that somehow he FELT that she was just the person for the place. He did not know, and I did not tell him, that he and she had been in touch mentally before they even met.

WHAT YOU ARE SEEKING IS SEEKING YOU

It is a law of the universe that what you are seeking is seeking you. In other words, if you have a very great desire and need for a certain thing there is someone who has that very thing for you. And that person is looking for someone of just your type to fill his need in his scheme of things. You would never have had that desire unless that thing had already existed for you. In fact, the thing is seeking you, and the desire on your part is merely the pull of it on your heartstrings. It cannot pull until you get onto the proper level. The person who is not fitted for that particular thing does not get a steady urging toward it. You felt the urge, therefore you were in a position to respond. And when you have come together with your desire there is mutual satisfaction. The other party is just as glad to have you fill that need as you are to get the financial returns from your job. You are fitted into a Divine plan of your life.

This holds true in business, marriage, social satisfactions—indeed in every department of life. Someone is looking for just your type as a life mate. You will meet when you hold the positive attitude. Someone wants you to work for him. He will pay you well. So hold to the thought that you are worth the larger salary you require. You will certainly make a contact with the right firm, at a proper price.

FOUR GREAT PRINCIPLES OF SUCCESS

It is good to visualise the thing you want, as the preceding chapter shows. But that is not all. We do not merely wish ourselves into anything we want. Action is needed, and courage. This is where the practical American business outlook comes in. The dreamer is often a failure, not because he dreams, but because he does nothing else but dream. The man who is wide awake is the only man who makes his dreams come true. It is a good thing to get our heads up into the clouds, for vision, as long as we keep our feet on the ground.

KNOW CLEARLY WHAT YOU WANT

The first great principle is the law of clarity. Know clearly what you want. This has been covered elsewhere in this book. Get a definite aim. The man who tries to get ahead without knowing clearly where he wants to go is like a hunter going out and firing promiscuously in the air. He will have a lot of excitement but few results.

Pick out a goal, or a job higher up. There may be someone filling that job right now. That doesn't matter. See it as your first goal. Devote fifteen minutes a day to the study of that job. See how you would improve upon the methods of the person now holding it. Read up in the public library everything you can about that particular thing. Become a master of that subject. Don't be bashful concerning your new knowledge. You do not have to rush around parading it, but when the opportunity offers make suggestions to your employer for the improvement of that particular thing. Of course you must not neglect your own job. Put in your best efforts at that. And suggest new ways of doing your own work as well. Employers are always on the lookout for men and women who will think beyond the limitations of their routine work. They like to see initiative.

CONCENTRATE YOUR EFFORTS

The second is the principle of concentration. Concentrate your efforts. Don't get too many irons in the fire. Don't be a "joiner." It is good to belong to a club or a lodge, but the man who spends a lot of his time on them has no energy left for his big aim in life.

Don't try to be too much of a good fellow. Most men and women who have gone far in their way have had to shut themselves off from a number of things that the average loser thinks necessary. There is a certain amount of self-sacrifice necessary to success, but the prize is worth it all. Many people talk about wanting success, but deep down in their hearts they really don't want it badly enough to pay the price for it. If it could be handed to them on a silver platter they would languidly reach out and accept it. But success is a prize, and prizes are not handed out for nothing. The athlete who has just broken a world's record knows that back of that supreme effort were long months of training, denying himself things he would have loved to eat, going to bed early while his companions were just starting out on an evening of pleasure, concentrating all his thought and effort on making himself supreme in his line.

Don't try to be a master of everything. Pick out the thing you feel you can master, and master it. This is an age of specialists. Specialize on your job.

Make it a rule to mix only with successful people. Choose your associates from among people who think success is possible, who think success, talk success. We absorb much more than we realize of the atmosphere with which we surround ourselves. You cannot afford to hang around with the fellow who is always complaining that there are no opportunities today, and who is full of reasons why he cannot get ahead. His reasons may all be valid, but you cannot win by listening to them.

Listen to the man who sees opportunity on every hand, and who is grasping them. Concentrate on the main idea, and leave the other ninety-five per cent of failures to absorb their own failure vibrations.

OPPORTUNITIES EVERYWHERE

There are always opportunities for the man whose eyes are open for them. You may be standing on one right now. But they do not come to us with a nice big label. They often are disguised. There are no opportunities for the man who is always complaining. But there are plenty for the man who is ready. We make our own opportunity. The world is alive and shrieking with opportunity. There's a continuous feast on. But the world is too busy to invite us. We have to wake up and find out where it is taking place. Others who are making good have no time to stop and tell us what to do. They shoulder us aside and go ahead getting their share. It is up to us to get our eyes open. Concentrate on them and you will see them.

Numbers of people used to walk into that church in Florence whose huge chandelier swayed back and forth. The majority saw it only as a danger, and hurried by lest it fall. But to one man it was an opportunity. Galileo walked in, studied the swing of the chandelier and from it worked out the principle of the pendulum, which became an integral part of clocks.

Thousands of men had lain under apple trees and had been struck on the head by falling apples. The majority sat up and rubbed their heads, then lay down again and slept through the warm afternoon. But to Newton the apple was an opportunity. When it struck him he commenced to wonder why it did not fall upward instead of downward, and from that he worked out the theory of gravitation, which has been at the basis of all our studies in physics.

For centuries men scraped themselves with blade razors, and cut themselves regularly, but did nothing about it. But one man saw a cut as his opportunity, and worked out the safety razor. He is a millionaire today.

For ages men dragged their shirts on over their heads, and became angry because it mussed their hair. But one man said, "Why shouldn't we have a shirt that goes on like a coat?" And he became rich.

San Quentin prison was full of men who had perhaps been no worse than thousands of others, but who had been caught at it. The majority spent their time figuring out new schemes for doing something unlawful and "getting away with it." But one man took his incarceration as an opportunity. He spent his time figuring out an entirely new system of merchandising, and when he came out he started a chain of stores which he sold out in three years for three million dollars.

The great growth of radio provides thousands of opportunities. Aviation is in its infancy. New systems of merchandising, new methods of production, new ideas in advertising. The coming of the 'bus lines. Indeed a thousand new opportunities are on every hand. Thomas Edison on his last birthday speech said the opportunities were greater than ever before. Your own handicap may be your very opportunity.

MAKE YOUR OWN DECISIONS

The third is the principle of decisions. Make your own decisions. Stand on your own feet. Think your own thoughts. Listen to the mature experience of others. Get their opinions on things. But cultivate the habit of making your own decisions. This is an essential to executive ability. No one else, no matter how successful or wise, can ever see into your problem and weigh all the factors as you can yourself. Far better to make an occasional mistake in judgment yourself than to be always right by following others' opinions.

HOW TO TRUST OWN JUDGMENT

In making any decision, first get all the facts. Write down all the reasons why you should go one way, and opposite them all the reasons for the other choice. After you have got them all down still search your mind for other reasons pro and con. Set these down until you cannot think of any more. Then set one off against the other. Weigh them carefully. Then draw your conclusion. Remember no one else has access to any store of wisdom that is closed to you. Big men got to the top by drawing on their own common sense. And gradually their judgment developed as they trusted it and tested it. They are not marvels, but they are game. After gathering the facts, and forming your decision, go ahead. Don't reconsider that decision. The human mind has a peculiar habit of wanting to reopen every decision. This must be fought. Some of the reasons you rejected in coming to that decision still clamor for recognition. They may be good reasons, yet they are outweighed. So shut them out and go foward with your plans.

To reconsider decisions is one of the most weakening habits anyone can get into. It saps the morale of anyone who indulges it. It makes for double-mindedness. It creates a wobbly character. Decisiveness is the jewel of a clean-cut character. Better to make an error of judgment now and then than to develop an indecisive character. So refuse absolutely to reopen the case. The only exception to this rule is when a certain course of action is plainly ruinous. Then the wise man will change it.

STAY WITH IT

The fourth principle is that of tenacity. Keep your face toward the goal, and hang on like grim death. Any successful man will tell you that success is not always a straight, smooth road. It is more often a series of ups and downs. The whiner stays down after a hard knock, but the winner gets up again and again. Remember, they can't lick you if you won't stay down. Times may come when you wonder if the prize is worth the pounding you are taking, and you are tempted to quit. Never quit under fire. No one is ever beaten until he himself lies down. As long as you get up and struggle ahead you are winning, whether you look like it or not. You may not be making as rapid progress as you would desire, but as long as you keep your eye on the goal you are winning. Swimmers crossing the English Channel never make a straight swim of twenty-two miles across the straits. They are carried this way by tides, that way by ocean currents. At times they are being carried away from the other shore, but long experience has taught them that they must expect to fight these tremendous forces, and face these disappointments and swim possibly forty miles before reaching the other coast. As long as they keep headed for the other side they are winning, no matter where the tide is carrying them.

So keep going when the going is hardest. People with the finest chances of success often quit just this side of their goal. A little more stick-to-it-iveness would have carried them to real success. Remember, it can't be hard all the time. It is bound to change. So you fight grimly on, and when you can no longer fight just hold on, refusing to stay licked. All the silent forces in the universe begin to pull for you. You place yourself in touch with fighters of the ages and draw new strength from them. And as sure as there is a God interested in the affairs of men, you will win, because God hates a quitter and gives the big things of life to those who don't know how to quit.

The spirit of the winner is exemplified in the following poem by Edgar A. Guest:

It is easy to quit! Anybody can say :—
"The hill is too high" or "it's too far away,"
Anybody can say :—"I'm too tired to keep on,"
And stop half way there, but don't you be that one.
Whenever life gives you a task hard to do,
Don't stop in the middle, but see the thing through.

It is easy to quit! Any fool can explain
To himself and his friends why the struggle was
    vain.
It doesn't take brains when you start cutting loose
From a difficult task to think up an excuse;
There is always a plausible, soul-soothing lie
On the tongue of the chap who refuses to try.

It is easy to quit and drop out of the game
And say you don't want either fortune or fame.
It is easy to pass up the chance to succeed,
To decide that a little is all you will need,

And leave to another the hard thing to do.
But it takes brains and courage to see the task
    through.

So boy, when you're tempted to quit or to shirk,
Remember a coward can run from his work,
A fool can give up, and he will when hard pressed,
But it calls for a man to go through with the test.
Keep on while you still have some strength to
    spend;
That is harder than quitting, but wins in the end.

A WINNING PERSONALITY

A winning personality is the most valuable asset any person can have. It is worth more than mere money, because it will attract money. Business flows in the direction of personality. It is worth more than mere beauty of face or form, because it will attract friends and hold them for all time. Charles S. Schwab was once asked what he considered the greatest asset a young person starting in life should have. Without a moment's hesitation he replied, "A winning personality." Mary Pickford is a beautiful woman, but it is not her beauty that has set her

apart from ten thousand other young women who
have sought success on the screen. It is her radiant
charm that cannot be stifled by the deadness of the
camera and the screen. As the years pass and Miss
Pickford loses the freshness of her beauty she will
still be America's sweetheart because she has the
faculty of drawing the love of those who see her,
even as the great Sara Bernhardt had in her old age.

Personality is difficult to define. It is that intang-
ible something that makes people like or dislike us.
It is to a person what the perfume is to a flower.
It must be a natural thing. Yet there is not one
person without a personality. Everyone can develop
himself and his natural gifts until he has a pleasing,
winning personality.

PERSONALITY vs. BEAUTY

A charming personality is more valuable than a
beautiful face. Surface beauty is desirable but it can
never hold its own in competition with charm.
Beauty is largely a gift of the gods, but charm is a
matter of personal development, and endures long
after beauty has passed away. A short time ago a
young lady in Edinburgh, Scotland, came to me at the
close of a lecture and said, "I am not conceited when

I say that I am more beautiful and have greater physical attraction than my sister, yet when I take my young gentlemen friends to our home they always lose interest in me and want to make their future calls on my sister." The reason was that her plain sister had found the secret of charm and could captivate these young men who had first been attracted by mere beauty. The young woman who would attract and hold the interest of the opposite sex can do it successfully if she will develop herself along the lines which we shall open up later in this book.

PERSONALITY INCREASES SALES

The salesman who develops a winning personality will always outsell his competitor. Other things being equal, the salesman whose personality attracts others will get the business. People buy from the salesman they LIKE. Anyone who can make friends can make customers. Personality opens doors that are slammed in the faces of other people. Many a salesman who finds it hard to get a hearing, and who cannot make a good impression during his first call, will increase his sales by studying his own personality and removing certain objectionable things. We shall see later how this is done.

Business is always attracted to the store or office whose occupants have a cheery, optimistic attitude. The human heart has a hunger for cheerfulness because it finds so much depression within itself. As a result, although the average individual does not stop to reason out his motive he does business with cheerful, happy people. The store that carries a happy, optimistic tone, whose clerks are happy-looking and obliging, will always get the major portion of the business in that city. Money and trade are negative things. They are always attracted to a positive atmosphere. Therefore, even when times are hard and business poor, the wise man never allows his customers to sense this. He should carry an air of prosperity and contentment. This cheerful attitude of itself helps turn the tide of depression and attracts business to his store.

BE YOURSELF

There are different kinds of successful personality, yet they all carry and convey the same underlying tone. Theodore Roosevelt was of the noisy, turbulent, enthusiastic kind. He was a "mixer" type. Lindbergh is at the opposite extreme: quiet, undemonstrative, shunning the spotlight as much as possible. There is the personality that is like a whirlwind, sweeping everything before it, and there is that one which is quiet and placid as a mountain lake. Yet underlying the two is the same inner steel-like strength. The big mistake many make is in thinking their own kind of personality is not attractive, and in trying to copy someone who is constructed altogether differently. And in copying they lose the essential strength and charm which make up their own individuality.

We are all different. No two of us are alike. Even our finger prints vary in minute details. Each of us is the product of a thousand generations. We have been thousands of years in the making. Each generation has added some particular characteristic or trait to our physical and mental make-up. There has gone into the web and woof of our personality a quality here and a mental slant there, so that this particular emotional and physical combination sets us definitely and distinctly apart from every other individual who has ever stepped onto this planet. No one else has ever had exactly the same combination of qualities that we have. Therefore we develop our own particular appeal to others by being ourselves, by cultivating those things through which Nature has differentiated us from all other humans.

THINGS THAT SPOIL PERSONALITY

In a lifetime devoted to the study of human nature I have found a great many unattractive kinds of personality. They can all be described in four different groups: the bombastic, the artificial, the cringing, and the "frozen" personality.

THE BOASTER

The bombastic personality is detested by everyone. No one likes the loud-mouthed, boastful person. There is a world of difference between self-confidence and boastfulness. Self-confidence is quiet and solid; boastfulness is noisy and empty.

THE CRINGER

At the other extreme is the cringing personality. The person who is so anxious to please—so afraid of offending others that he agrees with everything they say—is a "Yes" man. He makes himself a doormat and then is surprised that others walk on him. People take us largely at our own valuation of ourselves. And there are times when we must stand up for our principles or our rights, even though it means a decided disagreement with some strong-willed, dominating type of character. At any rate, it brings

60

our sincerity to the surface, and sincerity is one of the most important elements in a winning personality.

The Artificial

The artificial personality is seen in the affected person. There are some people who would rather be anything at all except themselves. They act, speak, look and walk artificially. They never are their natural selves until they are in their coffins, and then the people file by and say, "Doesn't he look natural." The waitress who takes your order with a bored air, as if she were a society lady just filling in time until her limousine called for her, is an example of this. The man who is nice to everyone outside his own home, but who shows his real meanness to his loved ones, is another.

Frozen Personality

One of the most unhappy personalities is what I call the "frozen" personality. It is usually found in men (but more often women) of the best mental and moral qualities, and it covers up all their desirable traits. There are splendid men and women, of high ideals and ambition, who are held back by bashfulness, timidity and reserve. They are the most misunderstood of all people. They like others and want to be on intimate terms with them. They have the most beautiful ideas and warm feelings toward their friends, but they do not dare let themselves out and be natural and spontaneous. They stifle back their natural impulses. They hold back from free, natural conversation in a crowd or with someone whom they like a great deal. They often have better ideas than those being expressed in a group, and could contribute a great deal in conversation that would be appreciated by others, but they shrink from "opening up." And very often their acquaintances toss their heads and say, " Oh, she is cold, aloof, stuck on herself," when all the time she may be most miserable in her reserve, wishing she could thaw out that personality and let others see the real person within.

MAKING OTHERS LIKE YOU

The secret of a successful personality is to make others like you, and desire your company. We must understand the springs of human nature, and know what others want before we can make our personality attractive to them. And now we come to the secret of making others like us.

Man is supposed to be a reasoning animal. It is true in a sense, yet ninety-five per cent of our reactions are instinctive, not reasoned. And we act and react according to whether we get pleasant or painful feelings from our varied experiences. We take instinctive likes and dislikes to others without reasoning why. But underneath all our contacts is what the biologist and psychologist calls the "Pleasure-Pain Theory."

PLEASURE-PAIN THEORY

Briefly, the pleasure-pain theory is that every living thing draws back from any experience that gives him a painful sensation, and comes back for more of any experience that gives him a pleasant sensation. Every living organism, from the tiniest bug to the greatest financier, reacts instinctively to pleasure or pain. Watch a dog in a home at which you are visiting. It knows a stranger is in the house. It comes to the door and looks inquiringly at the stranger. Past experience tells it that strangers sometimes give pleasure, sometimes pain. You speak a few kind words to it, and it wags its tail and comes a bit nearer, watching closely, however, for any hostile sign on your part. As you encourage it it comes and stands about the length of your arm away from you. You reach down and pat it, talking quietly to it meanwhile. When the dog finds that

63

you bring it pleasant sensations through stroking its back and head it comes back for more. And if you turn your attention from the dog to the conversation in the room it comes close and pushes its muzzle into your lap or hands. It wants more. It is responding instinctively according to the pleasure-pain theory.

As babies we may have been allowed to crawl about the floor. Seeing the pretty red-hot stove we touched it with a finger, but got a pain reaction. Thereafter we avoided that stove. But as we got to the stage where we could pull ourselves around the dining table by hanging on to its edge we may have got our finger in a sugar bowl or honey jar. As we put our finger in our mouths we got a sweet sensation that gave pleasure, so we cultivated that sugar bowl thereafter.

All our later reactions in life are conditioned on this theory. We draw back from the person who gives us an unpleasant sensation, and seek the company of those who give pleasure. The important question, therefore, is to find out what kind of treatment of others will make them seek our company.

Buried deep in every human heart is a desire to be recognized. The average man or woman does not know this, but it is there. The real inner person hungers for notice—to feel that he is not just one of millions of people, but a separate, distinct personality. When we recognize this we are well on our way to the development of a charming personality. This deep-seated desire for recognition is what causes us to dress differently. The man gets a particular necktie that he "likes." He does not know that he likes it because it gives him distinction. The woman buys a hat or a coat because it is different. As soon as she sees another woman with the same coat or hat she is disappointed. Her individuality is gone. We buy a home in a new addition. Every home is alike, built by the same contractor and sold on easy terms. But we want our walk, or our shrubbery, or our garden to be a little different from our neighbors. Why? We hunger for recognition.

Knowing of this fundamental desire in human beings the wise man or woman adapts himself to others, and works with them in such a way as to give them that sense of recognition. Here are some "Points in Personality Building" which will act as a guide of our conduct in winning others.

BE INTERESTED. Create a genuine interest in other people. The most unhappy people are those who are self-centered. We never find real happiness by being wrapped up in ourselves. Now for just one week let us determine that our interest will be in others. It is surprising how interesting other people become when we begin to look for the interesting things in them. I often stop and talk with a newsboy from whom I am buying a paper. I get a benefit from that contact, and the boy is glad that someone seems interested in him enough to talk. That ego, the inner self in him is crying out for recognition. When you show that interest it gives him a warm feeling within. He doesn't know why, but you do. And he likes you for it.

BE FRIENDLY. Meet people with a warm, friendly manner and a smile, as if to say, "I surely am glad to meet you." The good Book says, "A man to have friends must show himself friendly." That is not true because it is in the Bible. It is in the Bible because it is true. People sometimes say, "Well, I don't like so and so, and I cannot feel and act in a warm manner toward him." Yet if you were wandering around in Paris or Yokohama, alone in a crowd, you would greet your worst enemy with a warm handclasp. If you were shipwrecked on a desert island and this detestable person should come by in a boat you would find it easy to greet him warmly. We all have bumps that hurt and displease others. Perhaps you rub him up the wrong way by some of your mannerisms. Just act toward him as if you were cast on a desert island, and you will be surprised how he will warm up to you. After all, most people are pretty good at heart. The sharp corners are all on the outside, and underneath I have found most people at least as good hearted as I like to think I am myself.

The person who is grouchy may have some unseen reason for it. He may be carrying a heavy load. His business may be going to pieces, his health breaking down; there may be serious trouble in his family. He may be tangled in a habit that is breaking his heart. We can win his deepest friendship by refusing to act as everyone else does toward him. Give him friendliness and you produce the pleasant reaction and even though he does not reason it out he will like you and come back for more.

BE ACCURATE. It is surprising how touchy people are about their names. Mr. Browning is very much offended if you call him Mr. Brown. Get his name correctly. Get the details of his family affairs. You give a man a very warm pleasure reaction if, meeting him after an absence of three months, you say, "How is your boy's sore arm?" or show him in some other way that you have an accurate remembrance of certain details in his affairs. It is recognizing him as an individual apart. And it gives him a warmer feeling toward you.

BE SYMPATHETIC. Draw him out to talk about himself and his interests. When you meet a person he is not interested in you, your business, your family, your health, your affairs at all. Every person's chief interest is himself and his own affairs. The wise man will recognize this trait in human nature, therefore he will not start in to talk his own affairs, but will encourage the other to talk of himself. Draw him out to tell you of his business, to boast about his home town, his lodge, his flower garden, the cute thing his baby said. Let him stretch a point in telling you what distant station he got on the radio last night. Let him lie like a trooper over the size of the fish he caught while on his vacation. But listen well and let him do most of the talking. A good conversationalist is he who can say nothing at the right time. Let him feel your interest. You are making him feel that his affairs are important enough. You are giving him what he unknowingly craves — recognition. Don't let your attention wander. Look at him as he speaks. Don't make the mistake of thinking you have to look him in the eye. Many people are terribly embarrassed when you fix them with your eye. They are not crooks simply because they avoid your eye. Timid, sensitive people feel ill at ease when you look them square in the eye. You give them a painful raction. But

68

look somewhere at their face, perhaps the mouth, chin or nose as they talk, so that they see your sympathetic interest.

On the steamer going to Australia for our last lecture tour was a man who was an unmitigated bore. He harangued everybody about the Single Tax. If a group were sitting talking together and this man joined them first one and then another would make some pretext and leave the group, until he was left severely alone. I had never met the man until about five days out at sea I was up early one morning enjoying the morning air. There was no one else on deck so this man pulled his steamer chair over beside mine and started to talk. I had heard of him so I timed him by my wrist watch. He talked for two hours and forty minutes by the watch. And in all that time I asked exactly four questions. When he seemed to be running down I would prime him with another question and he would start off all over again. I learned a lot about the Single Tax that day.

That evening he said to a group of men in the smoking room, "There's only one intelligent man on this ship, and that is Dr. Bailes. I learned more from him in a little talk today than I've learned from any of you men." The poor soul didn't know that I hadn't contributed a thing except four questions. Here is the psychology of the incessant talker. He talks along, and doesn't notice that you are not joining in. He actually thinks of the things you ought to say to him, and keeps himself so busy answering them that he doesn't see that you haven't actually said them. And your sympathetic attitude gives him a warm, pleasant reaction. People have sometimes said to me, "Well, I simply would not try to be nice to a person like that." Well, that is the philosophy of the average man. If you want to be above the average you will take some pains to create pleasure in others. Of course I do not mean that a busy housewife or a business man could lay aside their work and listen for hours to people who run off at the mouth. There is a time and a place for everything.

BE THOUGHTFUL. Don't make wise cracks at the expense of others. You might get a laugh from the company assembled, but you've given an unpleasant reaction to the object of your joke. And he will avoid you. The kindly, thoughtful person will always have a host of warm friends because they know they feel secure in his company.

BE HONEST. Don't merely pretend all this interest and sympathy. Thoughts are things, and your thoughts register upon people, as well as the

70

words you say. If you are secretly despising another while pretending to like him. In other words if you are merely "working" him he may not be able to reason it out, but your aloof thoughts registering on his subconscious mind will give him an unpleasant sensation. And while he cannot say why he simply will not like you. Ring true in all your contacts with others. Sincerity is a jewel that will always be appraised at its real value.

BE TOLERANT. Don't try and make everyone else over into your own mould. This is especially true in matters of religion. One man is a Protestant and another is a Roman Catholic because he happens to be born and raised in a family of that faith. If either of us had been born in the other man's family we would have been just as devoted to that faith as he is. Each person has to work out his own theories of religion, and when you try to argue another into your way of believing you assault his individuality. You are failing to recognize his Ego. It does not mean that we should have no religious convictions, or that we should agree with ideas in which we do not believe. But the wise man says "Well, here is what I believe because it seems most reasonable to me. If you believe otherwise I shall give you credit for having as good judgment as I have. Stay where you are and I will stay where I am."

71

The same thing is true in regard to the private life of others. Don't criticize their habits. We may greatly disagree with their mode of living, but as long as they want to go that way we lose them by trying to win them. It is folly to try and argue a man away from alcohol, for example. As long as he wants it he will resent your efforts to keep him from it. The best way is to maintain a warm, friendly attitude toward him as a man. Show him you don't care for that habit, but that you like him in spite of it. Others are probably drawing their skirts closer to themselves as he passes by. He sees this and feels it. But he also knows that while you do not drink, nor approve of it, you do not treat him like a criminal because he does, and he likes you for it. You give him the pleasant reaction.

There always comes a time in the life of anyone who is held by a habit when he hates the habit and himself for indulging it. I believe the theologians call this the "rebound from sin." In the case of a drinker it comes after a hard spree. He wakes up and says "I hate this thing. I want to get away from it. Never again for me." At such a time he looks for someone to help him through it. To whom does he turn? Not to those who treated him like dirt. But to you. Then the advice you give has a hundred

times the weight it would have had if you had forced
it while he was unwilling to quit his bad habit.

BE HARD. Don't do too much for other people.
One of the surest ways to weaken your personality
is to be an easy mark. Why is it that those who
have given the best in themselves to others, who have
deprived themselves of necessities in order to give to
their children, often get no love or sympathy in
return. Parents who have sacrificed for their children are sometimes turned out of home in their old
age, or are placed in a charity home by ungrateful
children. The reason is that when you do too much
for others you make them hate you. In other words,
you make them feel inferior. They have not been
able to get things that they should have been able
to get through their own efforts, and you have to give
them to them. It makes them sense their inferiority.
This always gives them an unpleasant reaction. We
all have a duty to those about us to give them what is
fair. But when we become easy marks we hurt them
and us.

BE CHEERFUL. Finally, everyone is drawn to
the cheerful, happy individual. Robert Louis Steven-
son fought a life-long battle with tuberculosis, and
knew right along he was losing it. Yet he has written the most optimistic books possible. He knew

73

that while he had tragedy stalking him day by day in one form someone else had it in another form. And when you feel as if things are going too hard, and the tendency is to become bitter about it, just go out and take a look at the paralytics, the insane, and those whose outlook seems truly hopeless, and look up to your Creator with thankfulness that you have what you have. Everyone has a fight on his hands, and character is developed by the daily struggle. Allowing depression to enter never makes it easier to fight through, but choosing to smile and to take the courageous attitude will always make it a much shorter battle. No one or no thing can ever rob us of happiness but we ourselves. Nothing can ever touch the inner man until we let it in. We keep it out by affirming "I choose the happy outlook on life, and enjoy the little ray of sunlight I possess."

> *"Out of the night that covers me*
> *Black as the pit from pole to pole*
> *I thank whatever gods that be*
> *For my unconquerable soul."*

Success is a habit, just as failure is a habit. Most people have allowed themselves to get into the habit of expecting all the bad things to happen to them. But we can cultivate the habit of expecting the good instead. First thing in the morning when you awake, just lie there quietly and say "I wonder what good thing is coming into my life today. I wonder what good sale I will make, or friendship I will gain, or happy thing I shall experience." And last thing at night before dropping off to sleep just let the mind run over such words as "Love, Life, Beauty, Friendship, Courage, Confidence, Brightness, Cheerfulness, Optimism, Health, Happiness, Success." Don't try to think what they mean. Just think of the words without strain or effort of will. The Bible talks good psychology when it says "Whatsoever things are just, noble, pure, honorable, beautiful, think on these things."

DIFFERENCES BETWEEN SEXES

The natures of men and women are fundamentally different. And the reason why some men and some women fail to make any appeal to the opposite sex is that they do not understand these differences. Summed up, women like manliness in men, and men like womanliness in women.

WHAT WOMEN LIKE IN MEN

I have mentioned manliness as the sum total of what women like in men. This shows itself in many ways. And by taking the subject to pieces we can find out the essential things that go to make up this quality.

COURAGE

Courage ranks first among the manly virtues. A man may have ninety-nine good qualities, but if he is a coward he cannot hold the respect of a woman. This applies to physical as well as moral courage. The biggest part of Lindbergh's appeal to American womanhood lies in his sheer courage.

LEADERSHIP

Leadership is a form of courage. The man who has the habit of standing out from among the crowd; whose strength of character is shown in the willingness of others to follow him makes an instinctive appeal to women.

This same spirit of leadership will show itself in the ability to make up his mind. The man who is never sure of himself; who does not know which way to turn; who must always ask direction and advice of others before committing himself loses his hold over "the one girl." She likes him to be able to take

76

her into a good restaurant without showing signs of timidity. To act as if he were entirely at ease, and to make her feel the same when the eyes of others are upon them. She wants him to be able to help her make up her mind as to what she shall select from the menu, or to select it for her if she prefers. She wants him to be able to grab the one taxi on a rainy day when six different men are trying to attract the driver's attention.

A Go-Getter

He should be able to provide her with a good living. In these days when girls can make a good living for themselves they are not so anxious to marry the man who can only offer them himself and a life of near-poverty. This is not materialistic on the woman's part. It is wisdom. A man may not be making a large income at the time of marriage, but if he has shown that he is climbing he will make an appeal to the average young woman.

Behind this desire on the part of the young woman is a deeper psychological truth. A woman wants to be proud of her husband. Everybody loves the winner. Ask any middle-aged woman whose husband still earns the same amount he did when she married him. If she is confidential she will admit that it hurts her to hear other women telling of their husband's success while she has to remain silent, and cover up the fact that he is not a go-getter.

COURTESY AND THOUGHTFULNESS

Women are much more sensitive than men. They are more finely built. Things that a man throws off easily hurt a woman deeply. They appreciate the little courtesies of life. To open a door for her; to see that she is properly seated; to think of the "little things" often mean more to her than some things that the man thinks big. Many a woman whose husband brings home a diamond bracelet would far rather have him take her in his arms and tell her how much she means to him. She wants him to take her arm in a crowd, or crossing a street, to help her off with her coat in a public place, to pay her little attentions as he did when they were first engaged than she does to have him drive a new car up to the door and say, "It's for you." A box of candy, even if she is trying to reduce, or a bouquet of roses now and then mean more than some very expensive gifts. These little things show that he is thinking of her, and every woman always wants to feel that she occupies the front place in her husband's heart.

78

Optimism

No woman can love a grouch. Of course things go wrong at the office, but why spoil the home life by bringing the bad effects of business troubles home. The man worth while is the man who can smile when everything goes dead wrong. Many men keep their smiles for the outside world and then come home and "be natural." If you have only a few smiles keep them for those who love you.

Appreciation

Take note of the little things she has done to please you. The new hat, or the new hair wave, or the rearrangement of the living room. Don't always be crabbing over the gifts she does not possess. You are not so wonderful yourself, you know. Show her you appreciate the qualities she does have. When the one perfect woman is built every man will want her, but she has not been born yet.

Neatness

Keep yourself neat. A woman loves nothing better than to pull a hair off your coat collar, or to straighten a tie that is askew, because she wants you to be neat. Keep your linen clean. If you keep your-self "spruced up" you are paying her the greatest compliment possible. It is as much as to say, "I think a lot of your good opinion, and have taken pains with my personal appearance so as to please you."

ORIGINALITY

Think up new places to go, and new ways of en-tertaining. Know where you are going when you start out. Wandering around trying to think of something to do gets on a woman's nerves. Of course times come when both feel that they would rather start out for an aimless ride, but generally have an idea in mind regarding a definite place to go. There is nothing like the element of surprise to please people. So plan something different.

NO ROOM FOR JEALOUSY

Trust her. Don't allow any jealous streak to come in and shake your confidence. If you care enough for her to want her, and have decided that she can make you happy, have faith in her. Jealousy is a green-eyed monster that can ruin all happiness between the sexes. The jealous person can always see something that looks bad, even in a most innocent act. Every man and every woman who is in contact with the opposite sex at all will smile and pay attention to them. Yet it does not mean a flirtation. It is common social sense. Just because one woman gives her time or her affection to you it is unreasonable to ask that she shall immediately frown upon everyone else of your sex. You should be glad that others like to talk to her. If she loves you, trust her. And don't be a hog.

The jealous person is always a small person. And jealousy is an admission of it. You are jealous because you know that you are not large enough to hold the object of your affections. By being jealous you admit that someone else has more charm than you have; that you fear the attraction of some better person. And jealousy kills love because no one can respect a jealous man.

WHAT MEN LIKE IN WOMEN

Much of the foregoing applies to women as well as to men. Human likes and dislikes are very much alike. It is the purpose of this chapter to take up the essential differences in the sexes.

A Pleasing Voice

There is great charm in a rich, low voice in a woman. The shrill, high-pitched voices that many modern women affect grate horribly on the ears of the average man. Try to train the voice to a pleasing pitch. It is restful. And the big appeal of women to men lies in their ability to create an atmosphere in which men feel comfortable.

A Happy Smile

Men like a smiling woman. Not necessarily a toothy grin, which becomes monotonous. But the ability to break into a smile that takes in the eyes as well as the mouth. Nature has blessed women with his ability more than men. Watch a crowd getting on a street car or a train. Almost every woman comes walking down the aisle smiling as she looks for a seat. Let a woman trip over something on the sidewalk; she will usually cover her embarrassment with a smile. The man generally scowls at the obstruction, or kicks it out of the way.

And after a man has been battling with the world all day, a smiling, happy reception as he arrives home makes him feel that it is a pretty good old world after all. It is sometimes hard to smile, when everything has gone wrong in the home all day. The woman thinks the man should know all about the home cares, but here is a secret, ladies. The average man is so taken up with his own worries he fails to realize you have your own. So deny yourself the privilege of telling him all about it. Push your own troubles aside and smile. Listen to his tale of woe, if he has to tell it. Sympathize with him. Tell him what you think of those unkind people who hurt his feelings. Later you can bring out your own problems, but keep the happy side forward until after he has eaten.

GENTLENESS AND WOMANLINESS

Woman's appeal to men lies in her femininity. Her voice is softer, her flesh is softer, and in this lies much of her charm. Keep the disposition gentle and yielding. Don't make wise cracks at his expense especially when he is irritable. No woman has to give in continually to a man and make herself a doormat. But tactfully she can get her own way in round about methods. To stand up and fight him for what she wants will always arouse his antagonism.

HERO-WORSHIP

Every man likes to think he is a hero. The world in general does not recognize his heroic qualities. So he warms up to the one who does. Lead him to feel that you think he is wonderful. Listen to his plans, his accomplishments, his theories of the way Hoover should arrange farm relief. Keep yourself well posted on the kinds of things he is interested in, so that you can discuss them intelligently with him. But let him feel that when he gives an opinion there is good sense to it. The flapper trick of looking up with adoring eyes into the young man's face (or into the old man's face) and breathing "Oh, you are so-oooooo wonnn-derrrr-fulllll" is based on the best knowledge of masculine psychology. Even though he feels she is not wholly sincere in it he likes to hear it. Men are vain. I am a man.

MODESTY

We hear a good deal these days about the loss of modesty in women. If women lose their modesty it will be the greatest tragedy the world has ever seen. Because they will lose the greatest pulling power they possess. No matter how much a man of the world he may be every man instinctively responds to modesty in women. It intrigues him. And modesty is a thing of the heart, not the clothes. A young woman may wear the very latest styles in clothing, and carry a mind that is as unsullied as a flower.

The outcry against short skirts comes from unclean minds. Woman has from past ages been a possession of man. They kept her for their own use, as they would a horse or any other chattel. They shut her away behind walls, they made her cover her face, they made her reveal nothing of those charms which they alone owned in her. But that day is rapidly passing. Woman is coming into her own. She is dressing for comfort and attractiveness. She belongs to no man. Her body is not an indecent thing. It is man's thoughts about that body that are often indecent. And whether the legs are covered or uncovered the mind of man can imagine all he wants to.

There is nothing more æsthetic than a pair of well-shaped legs in a pair of silk hose. And there is certainly nothing indecent in the bare legs of the new stockingless fashion. The indecency lies in the prurient minds of those who are shocked by an exhibition of skin.

The one-piece bathing suit has come in for its share of horrified stares and outcries from filthy-minded people who belong to reform societies. I am writing this book while I summer in Long Beach, California, where the Creator has combined the finest of his art in climate, beach, ocean and general surroundings. This glorious three-mile beach front is crowded with bathers. And the perfection of creation is the healthy, normal ladies of all ages who are garbed in the one-piece suit. Force them into the baptismal robes that they bathed in fifteen years ago and you haven't changed their minds, nor the minds of the men who bathe with them. Modesty is of the mind, not the clothing.

We spent part of last summer in the South Sea Islands. There the natives bathed with as little clothing as possible — certainly less than the one-piece suit. Yet their morals are no worse than the morals of white men and women.

Dress as you like, but keep your mind clean. The girl who allows familiarity with the opposite sex cheapens herself and loses her hold upon the very men who cheapen her.

86

NEATNESS

Keep yourself and your home neat. The woman who allows the dishes to pile up in the kitchen sink; who never can find a thing she is looking for; who has her home looking as if a cyclone had just passed through it; who allows the children to run around untidy; who hands a man his underwear with three buttons missing is bound to lose her charm for him.

There are, of course, many other elements that enter into the case, both from the man's and the woman's side, but these will serve as a starter. Others will develop as you work out your own problem. Follow out the fundamental principles laid down in the chapters on personality building, and make every line of conduct square with the rules set forth there. I commend to you a little poem written by Thomas Bracken, the New Zealand poet, and given to me by his son Charles Bracken, a member of one of my classes in New Zealand last year.

NOT UNDERSTOOD

Not understood; we move along asunder
Our paths grow wider as the seasons
Creep along the years; we marvel and we wonder
And then we fall asleep—
    Not understood.

Not understood; how trifles often change us
The thoughtless sentence or the fancied slight
Destroy long years of friendship, and estrange us
And on our souls there falls a freezing blight—
    Not understood.

Not understood; poor souls with stunted vision
Oft measure giants with their feeble intellect;
The shafts of falsehood and derision
Are oft impelled 'gainst those who mold the age—
    Not understood.

Ah God! That men would see a little clearer
Or judge less harshly where they cannot see
Ah God! That men would move a little nearer
One another—they'd be nearer Thee—
    And understood.

Made in the USA
Monee, IL
06 January 2023

24659110R00052